# How to Write a Book in 48 Hours

A Simple Step-by-Step System for Writing a Good Book Fast

## Dale L. Roberts

One Jacked Monkey LLC

## Disclaimer

# The DIY Publishing Course for Beginners

Are you ready to begin your self-publishing journey?

You have a story.

It deserves attention.

Learn the fundamentals of self-publishing books...

In this in-depth, yet succinct, course.

It's perfect for anyone new to the self-publishing business!

It will take you from manuscript to self-published.

The best part? It's 100% free!

Visit DIYPublishing.biz/Free to enroll today.

# Table of Contents

# Introduction

E ver since I was a boy, I have wanted to be a writer. My sudden transition from the world of the young adult book series *The Hardy Boys* to Stephen King's *The Tommyknockers* was the start of my lifetime obsession with reading and writing. King's imaginative writing and crafty storytelling made me believe I could share the same quality material, but with a unique spin. I would spend hours reading his books, then even more hours writing similar stories. In each story, I would pen my nightmares into intricate landscapes or my greatest dreams into feel-good moments.

The older I became, the less confident I was in my abilities. Every story I started, I never finished. Most of the time, I would find myself stuck in editing mode. I could hardly get past my first sentence. Other times, I had the intent to write interesting content only to stop. My belief was I just didn't have the time to accomplish a work as great as my favorite author. If I couldn't write a book worthy of my writing hero, how could I ever finish my work?

In due time, I would start story after story until I had stacks of unfinished stories. Even now, I have scads of material and unfinished projects, but these days I'm not being hampered by my stinking thinking. After reading many systems put into place by successful authors, I developed my system for writing books. Now, nothing is holding me back.

Time is no longer an excuse I can use to stop writing. I have this writing process down to a science. Now, I want to share what has made me successful in putting pen to paper and creating good books fast.

People want to write a book to share their story, but they think they don't have the time to do it. Sometimes, people believe they have to be an expert writer or have a college degree to complete a book. Worse yet, a few people believe they have nothing of value to share. These excuses are furthest from the truth. I'm happy to tell you why in *How to Write a Book in 48 Hours: A Simple Step-by-Step System for Writing a Good Book Fast.*

First, let's focus on what the definition of what a book is, according to Merriam-Webster:

> *book - A set of printed sheets of paper that are held together inside a cover; a long-written work; a long-written work that can be read on a computer.*[1]

The belief that a book is long-written work is enough to scare away any hobbyist, since it implies a mountainous task in the undertaking. Today's standards have changed for the writer because of the modern reader's expectations. The new bibliophiles are not just looking for the next epic *War & Peace* novel. They are seeking bite-sized books they can easily read and digest as quickly as possible.

Previously, writers had to spend years crafting a genius creation and then find a book deal with a large publishing house to be successful. Many talented writers never had their books seen by larger audiences due to lack of knowledge or connections.

Writing a book is different today, because of technology. Now you write a book with ease through a few different ways - typing, talk-to-text, and outsourcing. Then, you have it edited and proofread by website applications or online freelancers. Lastly, you publish it. If you put this book down right now, I have every bit of confidence in you to Google-search ways to get the job done with what I have given you. But what I will offer is some insight into what has and has not worked for me as a self-published author.

# YOUR FIRST STEPS

After each chapter, I'll give you the practical steps and a few additional tips that'll help grease your creative wheels and get you rolling out your next book. Though each of these items seem trivial, give them a shot. You just might surprise yourself.

## PURPOSE PONDERING

- ○ Clarify the purpose of your book.
- ○ Identify what you want readers to gain.

## AUDIENCE ASSESSMENT

- ○ Define your target audience.
- ○ Consider their demographics and preferences.

## GENRE REFLECTION

- ○ Decide between fiction and nonfiction.
- ○ Identify your passion and strengths.

## NOTES

# Setting a Timeline

Estimated time to complete: ~5-10 minutes

S ince you have 48 hours to complete a book, you must remove any distractions or obstacles. You need nothing hindering your focus on this book project. Designate a date, time, and location for you to complete this project. If you have a nine-to-five job, then you should choose a weekend, so you finish the entire project in one fell swoop. However, if you don't have the discretionary time, then split up your work as your schedule permits.

Work on your project in 90-minute increments, then take a quick break. If you have the energy and work ethic to continue without a break, then kudos to you. I recommend taking slight breaks to keep your head sharp.

I break up my projects with meals, snacks, workouts, and small household chores. My breaks never last longer than 30-60 minutes at a time.

Devote a majority of the 48 hours to the writing process. I spend nearly 18 hours in a day (with breaks included) writing. I know other self-published authors who spend far less time and produce superior content. It's up to you how much time you spend on your project.

# PRACTICAL STEPS

Time management is critical to the success of your book writing efforts. The difference between writing a book in 48 hours and 48 days is how you manage your time. Reflect back on the points made in this chapter, then tackle your next steps as listed below.

## DEADLINE DECISION

○ Choose a realistic finish date.
○ Visualize the sense of accomplishment.

## SETTING GOALS

○ Set achievable targets.
○ Celebrate small victories for motivation.

## CONSISTENCY COMMITMENT

○ Schedule dedicated writing time.
○ Stay flexible and adapt to changes.

## NOTES

# Two Ways to Write Content

An enormous part of creating content is becoming resourceful with what you have. Whether you can type, talk, or have cash flow, you can produce a book. All you need to do is pick a path you are most comfortable with for producing your book. There are two ways I prefer, and they include:

- Typing & Writing

- Voice dictation

Typing—or writing—is the old-fashioned method I prefer over other ways of producing a book. For me, touch-typing comes easy since I took typewriting classes in high school. This skill has been an asset and has improved over the years.

If you can't type or aren't very good at it, there are plenty of ways you can learn this skill. Take online courses or even use website applications to fine-tune your typing.

Learning how many words per minute you type gives you an idea of your current skill level. Regardless of the limited experience you have, you should still see how many words you can type. Use the Type Speed Test (visit DaleLinks .com/TypeTest) to see how many words per minute you type. The test is one minute, and you get a reasonably accurate representation of where your abilities lie. You receive recommendations on how to improve from the test.

Test your skill to see if you can realistically type a short book in 48 hours. If you can type 50-80 words per minute (wpm), you could write a 10,000-word manuscript within 2-4 hours. This word count comes out to roughly 25-40 pages, based on the formatting.

For a rough idea of your manuscript size and how to best classify your work, you can refer to these guidelines:

- Short Story = 1,000 to 8,000 words

- Novelettes = 7,500 to 20,000 words

- Novellas = 20,000 to 50,000 words

- Novels = 70,000 to 90,000 words

- 250 words = 1 page[1234]

The online writing resources mostly agree with these word counts, but nothing is set in stone. These word counts are general guidelines, meaning the content makes the book, not the word count. If you are looking to self-publish, these guidelines are helpful, but, again, nothing you need to adhere to strictly.

Look into the industry average for the niche you are writing (i.e., science fiction, fantasy, horror, etc.) if you wish to submit your work to publishers. Literary agents and publishers have strict criteria for content, and if you don't meet them, they won't even look at your manuscript.

Nonfiction is based on content more than word count. If you provide factual insights, you don't need to fluff it up with unnecessary content. Otherwise, you may lose your readers and any credibility you are building in your niche. Stick to the facts and create a solid book you can confidently stand behind.

## Voice Dictation

Voice dictation is the second-best viable option when it comes to writing books. If your typing isn't great and you don't want to learn, then dictation is your solution for writing a book. Supposing you have an inner editor slowing you down, then this is an excellent solution for you. This process is a lot easier than you'd think. It requires a few different tools than traditional writing:

- Recording device

- Speech recognition software—aka speech-to-text

This type of writing involves your ability to speak. I tried both types of voice-to-text writing and had mixed results. My favorite of the two is a recording device.

## Recording Device

Any recording device will do, but it is in your best interest to use something modern or digital. Using more recent technology will get you a product quicker than outdated analog technology (i.e., tape recorders, camcorders, etc.). The process is simple:

Record yourself discussing your content. Essentially, you write your book by talking it out.

Get your recorded material transcribed by a professional or a proficient typist.

I used a transcriptionist on Fiverr (DaleLinks.com/Karen), who charged me $5 for 30 minutes of audio content (roughly 3,500 words). After eight orders of

30 minutes apiece, I invested about $40, plus platform fees. To date, the short read earned over $1948 in revenue across ebook, print book, and audiobook.

Here are a few ideas for getting a transcriptionist:

1. Use my preferred transcription service called Rev (DaleLinks.com/Rev). They come at a higher premium, but they guarantee quality. Also, you can translate your work and produce even more from one piece of content.

2. Hire someone on Fiverr.com to get it done. It's nice to get your work done cheaply and quickly. Shop around for the right option for you.

3. Hire a freelancer on Upwork.com or any similar website. The beautiful part about posting work on a freelance site is you can name your price. Most times, the website safely holds your money in escrow until your freelancer completes the project. Hire someone according to your deadline and your budget.

4. Find a college or high school student needing a little work.

5. Ask a friend or family member who is proficient at typing.

When the option is available to get it done for free, go for it! Just make sure your transcriptionist can produce your work in a timely fashion.

When hiring a freelancer, be sure you:

- Are familiar with their work history

- Have reviewed samples of their work

- Can trust this person

- Set specific expectations

- Use a secure transaction for your money—any money-back guarantee, fraud protection, escrow, and more

## Speech Recognition Software

I have limited experience with speech recognition software, but I tested Dragon Naturally Speaking (version 12.5). The program cost me $25 and included the software, updates, and headset. It took some time to "train my dragon" so the software recognized my voice pattern and dialect. I didn't have too many issues or errors when I spoke into the headset and found few mistakes. The more I used the program, the fewer mistakes and misinterpretations I made.

There are a few other voice recognition programs on the market, so research your options prior to starting your project. A few phone and computer applications have voice recognition programs with mixed results and reviews. Before you talk for hours on end into a voice-to-text program, make sure it accurately transcribes. Otherwise, much of your time will include fixing errors, interpreting what you said, or re-wording awkward sentences.

I used Google Docs with my mobile phone to dictate some short stories. Much like Dragon, speak slow, verbalize relevant punctuation, and speak any commands (i.e., next line = hard enter).

In due time, technology will advance enough that typing might become the second most used medium for producing content in books. For now, be careful using speech recognition for writing.

# PRACTICAL STEPS

Admittedly, if your writing skills aren't very sharp, you'll need plenty of practice before cranking out a book in two days. Everyone has limitations, so I can't possibly prescribe what works best for you. Forty-eight hours might not be enough time for you. Nonetheless, assess your speed for each process to see what method is most efficient. With practice, you'll go faster and grow more confident.

## TYPING & WRITING

- ○ Assess typing speed for productivity.
- ○ Explore online typing courses.

## VOICE DICTATION

- ○ Utilize recording devices for dictation.
- ○ Explore speech recognition software.

## NOTES

# How to Choose Your Topic

Estimated time to complete: ~30-60 minutes

T he first step in writing a book is the hardest. First, figure out what you are going to write about in your book. Deciding a topic seems easy enough but much tougher in practice. Let's start with two options of writing:

*fiction - Written stories about people and events that are not real; literature that tells stories that are imagined by the writer; something that is not true.*[1]

*nonfiction - Writing that is about facts or real events; all writing that is not fiction.*[2]

Choose the option that best suits you. Before you pick the type of book, think about what you are strongest and most passionate about sharing. For instance, if you like talking about your dreams in vivid detail, then you may be a person who has a creative edge on everyone. You could easily fit into the genre or style of writing for fiction. The half-hour you share your dream with someone, you could easily write part of a book.

If you are passionate about a hobby or vocation, then you are perfect for the nonfiction genre, a style of writing that expresses something true. I excelled in the nonfiction genre because of my experience in personal training and self-publishing. The funny thing is I don't show any signs of letting up on these particular niches or subcategories of nonfiction. I write nonfiction books because I have a lot to share and I'm passionate about topics like fitness and self-publishing.

When you choose what you want to write about in your books, be sure you like what you write. Otherwise, it becomes a tedious chore, and you are bound to become easily distracted. Get enough distractions, and a book project can go from being produced in 48 hours up to 48 months. When you choose a subject of interest, the book project will roll along smoothly, and you are more susceptible to staying on track for a quick finish.

Once you know the type of book you're writing, determine your target audience. Visualize your readers and specifically who they are. You won't speak to an older adult the same as you would a toddler. Or you wouldn't write a guitar repair manual for a car mechanic. A few things to consider when choosing your audience are their demographic or their:

- Age

- Gender

- Geographic location

- Income level

- Education level

- Occupation

- Marital or family status

- Ethnic background[3]

Choose your words carefully and read aloud to be sure you are speaking in a way you would to the audience you are targeting. In fact, if you try to win every audience, you will get no audience in return. Pick your ideal readership and speak directly to them.

Find authors who write to an audience you are most interested in working with in your writing. Study these authors and find out what is making them most successful. Then, try to duplicate their same voice without plagiarizing their content or property.

# PRACTICAL STEPS

When you're ready to write a book in less 48 hours, lean on what interests you most or something you have deep insights and knowledge in. Writing isn't always have to be about chasing after the hottest trend to make a quick buck. Walk the path of least resistance when choosing a topic or story that you know well.

## FICTION OR NONFICTION

- ○ Reflect on personal strengths and passions.
- ○ Consider your creative edge.

## TARGET AUDIENCE VISUALIZATION

- ○ Define reader demographics.
- ○ Tailor your writing style accordingly.

## NOTES

# How to Pick a Title

P icking a title for your work can be fun and easy, but first, consider success-ful titles used by other books. You shouldn't steal another author's title, more so, model your title according to those successful authors.

Use Amazon as your search tool for finding the bestselling titles on the market. Amazon is a tremendous search engine people use a lot, so you can find successful books quickly. Based on one word typed into the search bar, Amazon auto-suggests other common word combinations searched on their site. For instance, if you type "exercise," then Amazon may suggest:

- Exercise and fitness

- Exercise physiology

- Exercise books

- Exercise motivation

- Exercise over 50

*The suggested keywords change over time. Check back later and you'll find a different set of keywords.*

The possibilities change based on what you add to your first word. This kind of search is a quick way to see what people are looking for on Amazon. Limit your search to Amazon's Kindle Store or Books, so you aren't getting suggestions for other products outside of literature.

Now, click on a book related to your niche. Scroll down on the product page and view the Best Sellers Rank under Product Details. You will see Amazon lists the book in 1 to 3 subcategories. Click on the category relevant to your book. The website redirects you to the Top 100 books of that niche.

*The Amazon Best Sellers List for Quick Workouts.*

Focus on the first 10-20 books in the Top 100 books. Open each page to see the title, book description, reviews, and any other information. When you gain a better sense of what is currently successful, you can choose a title that will cater directly to your audience.

You may see a recurring word, a combination of words, or a common theme among the top titles in your niche. Try to embody the best of all the concepts while still honoring the book you are producing. Write down as many repeated words as you can, and then choose the best words from that list to form an interesting title.

When you develop a few rough titles, pick out one that works best for you. Would you pay to read this book without seeing the cover? Is the title strong enough to entice you to buy the book? Does the title evoke an emotion or stir interest in you?

Spend only a half-hour on this step, and then set the title off to the side. It's not set in stone yet, and you can always tweak this title when you are ready to put the finishing touches on the book. Starting with a title establishes the desired tone for your book. It keeps your focus razor-sharp and directly aimed at the finished product that represents the manuscript best.

A broader way of researching the popularity of a niche is by using Google Trends to compare keywords and terms. This way, you can see what people are more apt to search. A graph representing the search trend over the past few years will show each word's performance in the search engine. Go to Google Trends to compare keywords and their performance. That way, you pick ideal words most likely to be looked up by your audience.

For example, type in the search window "exercising" and "working out." Insert a comma between the words for Google to differentiate between terms or words for an accurate search. People have consistently searched for "exercising" for the past decade, according to my findings. Whereas "working out" is being increasingly sought over the last ten years, making it the stronger performer of the two researched words.

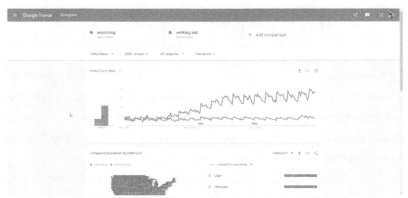

*Google and the Google logo are registered trademarks of Google LLC, used with permission.*

Google Trends goes further about the keyword and how well it performs throughout the world. Terms and words related to the searched word appear further down on the page. This tool merely helps enhance the quality of your title and not just a shiny object designed to distract you from finishing your book.

Ultimately, the title you choose is up to you. If you are providing quality content in your book, then the title will be secondary. When you consistently produce excellent books, you will build an audience of raving fans. Remember, you can always change your title or even repurpose your published book later if the title doesn't sit well with you.

# PRACTICAL STEPS

Coming up with a title is easy for some, but for the vast majority of aspiring authors, it's no small feat. If you're stuck and don't know what your title should be, study other books in your niche. Rest assured, you are not obligated to keep the title and can change it later.

## AMAZON EXPLORATION

○ Use Amazon to find bestselling titles.
○ Analyze titles in your book's niche.

## GOOGLE TRENDS COMPARISON

○ Utilize Google Trends for keyword popularity.
○ Select ideal words for potential searches.

## NOTES

# How to Outline Your Book

Estimated time to complete: ~30–60 minutes

T he next step is to write or type out a general outline of your book. Just focus on the main points you want to communicate. When you open your book, what would appear in your table of contents? These main points later become my chapters.

Don't worry about editing, organizing, or formatting until later. Just go with your flow of thought and keep your inner editor at bay. Now is the time for uninhibited ideas, so just let whatever comes out spill onto your page without interruption or judgment.

Once you have your key points laid out, ask relevant questions about each one. As an example, when I'm writing a book on exercise, I may have key points like this:

- Squats

- Push-ups

- Pull-ups

Then, I ask questions about each key point:

1. Squats

    a. What are squats?

    b. Why are squats important?

    c. Who can do squats?

    d. How do I perform a squat?

    e. What can I expect when I squat?

    f. Are there alternatives to squats?

2. Push-ups

    a. What are push-ups?

    b. Why are push-ups important?

    c. Who can do push-ups?

    d. How do I perform a push-up?

    e. What can I expect when I do push-ups?

    f. Are there alternatives to push-ups?

3. Pull-ups

    a. What are pull-ups?

    b. Why are pull-ups important?

    c. Who can do pull-ups?

    d. How do I perform a pull-up?

e. What can I expect when I do pull-ups?

f. Are there alternatives to pull-ups?

This example is a rather dry presentation of how I outline a nonfiction book, but still useful. Sometimes, I will break down each of the questions into smaller questions, giving the most comprehensive approach to my subject.

For fiction, I start from the back by developing an effective ending. Then I write the most impressionable beginning to hook the reader. Here is how I outline my fiction:

- Chapter 3 - The villain gets his comeuppance.

- Chapter 2 - The villain overcomes the hero.

- Chapter 1 - The villain swindles the hero.

Now I write out relevant characters, their traits, and their part in the story. For instance:

- Christopher - the hero, 29-year-old firefighter, philanthropist

- Judas - the villain, 18-year-old misfit hooligan, thief

After I know who is in the story, I can build more of a story around them. Like I do in nonfiction, I ask questions to paint a better picture or state what happens. Just like this:

- Chapter 3 - The villain gets his comeuppance.

  ○ Judas turns his back, long enough for Christopher to get the upper hand; what happens?

  ○ Christopher gets wounded by his captor but gets the upper hand. What happens to Judas after the authorities apprehend him?

  ○ The story finishes with Christopher fulfilling his obligation to the fundraiser and being recognized for his brave act of valor. What happens to Judas?

- Chapter 2 - The hero is being overcome by the villain.

  - Christopher confronts Judas; what happens?

  - Judas pulls a gun on Christopher and holds him up for more valuables. What is Christopher thinking about doing? How does he react to Judas when physically abused at gunpoint?

  - What is crossing Judas's mind as this occurs? Does he have any attributes worth relating to in this story? Or does he commit despicable acts that make us cheer for our hero? What are those acts, and why?

- Chapter 1 - The villain swindles the hero.

  - Christopher is preparing for a big fundraiser for the local children's hospital. How does Judas prevent this from happening?

  - How will Christopher react when he cannot fulfill his obligations to the fundraiser? What are his first actions when he finds out he cannot do a thing about it?

  - Why is Judas preventing this from happening? What is he gaining from stopping this fundraiser? Why doesn't he want the same thing as Christopher?

You can clearly work this example, a generic storyline, in so many ways. I have a general idea of what I want to convey in my story. If I want to expand more, I could ask questions about the setting, the physical attributes, and the motives of each character.

Once you have your completed outline, reorganize any key points into a hierarchy or order of importance. In nonfiction, this process will be much easier to handle. Fiction will be more difficult, so don't get stuck on it too long. You can always iron out the order of importance later when you write the content.

# PRACTICAL STEPS

An outline is critical for writing any good book fast, especially if you're doing it in two days. If you don't like the pressure of an outline, create one that fits your unique writing style. Should you deviate from the outline when you're writing, it's okay. Just go with the flow.

## MAIN POINTS IDENTIFICATION

- ○ Outline key points for chapters.
- ○ Envision the table of contents.

## QUESTION EXPANSION

- ○ Ask detailed questions for each point.
- ○ Ensure a comprehensive approach.

## NOTES

# How to Write Your Book

Estimated time to complete: ~3-6 hours or more

Now it's time to write your book. It's as simple as answering your questions. When answering, be as descriptive as possible. Think of your audience as new to the experience, so you should spare no detail.

Reflect on your favorite authors and the aspects you admire about them. Try to duplicate their process of presenting facts or setting a scene. Just do it in your words. Don't worry about how you say it when you are writing. Just write the story with a flow of thought.

As with all first drafts, write the story, then make corrections after you are done. Save any errors, plot holes, typos, grammatical errors, and word usage until after completing your work.

In *Everything You Need to Know About Writing Successfully – in Ten Minutes*,[1] Stephen King states you shouldn't use reference books when you are first writing. If you look up a better word or correct spelling, it can be a slight distraction that may derail you and leave you with writer's block. Instead, always go with your flow of thought and don't question what you write until after you are done. From personal experience, it is best to get it out and edited later.

Think of your writing as a different way of talking. You never have the chance to edit or amend what you say until after the fact. When speaking, you just get whatever is on your mind out into the air. Then, if you say something undesirable, you can always correct yourself.

Once you answer all the questions, you should have a pretty good rough draft and be ready to jump into the next process.

## How to Create a Book with Voice-to-Text

Once you have your outline for your book written, get your recording device ready. Test run your technology to make sure it works correctly, and you can hear your voice well enough for transcription. If you are using speech recognition software, then speak a few sentences to make sure it is capturing what you are saying accurately. Do not skip testing your technology, because you 'don't want to repeat this process.

Much like traditional writing, answer the questions from your outline. When talking, spare no details. It's better you say too much than not enough. It's easier to go back and remove extraneous material than it is when you have to add missing content.

Don't worry about stutters, filler words, or unimportant babbling you do throughout the process. It'll happen, so don't fight it. Once again, it's easier to remove unnecessary content than it is to add missing points. Be confident in what you share, speak clearly and succinctly.

The most paramount rule in the voice-to-text process is to isolate yourself completely. You don't want any barking dogs, screaming children, or phone calls. Tell everyone in your home you will be busy during your chosen time and shouldn't stop you during the process. If you express how important it is to you, they will understand.

The last step in this process is to get your material transcribed. Refer to the previous chapter on *Two Ways to Produce Content*. If you have speech recognition software, you should have a rough draft ready once you finish speaking.

# PRACTICAL STEPS

Time to get to work. Now comes the hardest part of the entire process: writing the first draft. Follow the prompts below and get to work. Good luck!

## AUTHOR REFLECTIONS

- ⚪ Reflect on favorite authors' aspects.
- ⚪ Emulate effective writing styles.

## DESCRIPTIVE DRAFTING

- ⚪ Answer questions with descriptive details.
- ⚪ Imagine the audience as newcomers.

# CREATING A BOOK WITH VOICE-TO-TEXT

## EQUIPMENT TESTING

- ⚪ Ensure recording and speech recognition functionality.
- ⚪ Familiarize yourself with chosen technology.

## DETAILED DICTATION

- ⚪ Answer outline questions with elaboration.
- ⚪ Allow natural flow; worry about errors later.

# Edit & Proofread Your Book

Estimated time to complete: ~6-8 hours or more

I would love to think I have the superpower to produce quality content with the first draft. Even the best writers have to edit their work before a publishing company will release it. I can't afford the same quality editing as contracted authors from big publishing houses, so I make do with what I have.

Before I share how I perfect my work, it's important first to understand what editing is. The primary duties of editing a book are:

- Punctuation, capitalization, spelling, and grammar

- Improper word usage

- Subject-verb agreement

- Use of passive/active sentence structure

- Consistency in treatment of material

- Style and formatting of the content

- Accuracy of citations, references, notes, tables, figures, and charts

- Ambiguity, incorrect statements, lapses in logic, libelous comments[1]

I feel most comfortable running at least two rounds of edits to ensure I have missed no details. Before you send your work off to an editor, read through your book and perform the first edit. I use an excellent online editing tool called ProWritingAid (DaleLinks.com/ProWritingAid). This application helps with:

- Plagiarism checking

- Grammar

- Proofreading

- Style-specific editing

- And a few more cool features

The free version of ProWritingAid is sufficient for basic copyediting, while the premium version is much more robust with features and reports.

When you do the next edit, it's best to use an unbiased, outside source. You can easily overlook mistakes, so getting an outside perspective brings a fresh set of eyes to your project. If you use an outside party for editing, you are bound to get a more quality finished product.

If you lack the finances to pay for editing, try to reach out to anyone within your network of friends, family, or colleagues. It amazes me how many people will help an aspiring author. Be warned, though, you are at their mercy if you are not paying for their services. And if they don't have a background in editing, you may not get the best results. You may get a better edit done with them than without them.

I hired editors through Upwork before with mixed results. The pay rate for an editor can range from $0.005 to $0.10 per word. A 10,000-word document can cost from $50 to $1,000 for an editor. Before you hire an editor, make sure they have a background and some experience in editing. You will get what you pay for, so choose wisely.

Make any corrections as you see fit. Sometimes you may not agree with your editor's notes, but you should at least entertain what they suggest. Once you make all the corrections and read through your book again, you are ready to proofread.

Proofreading is another task that works best when you bring in an outside perspective and try to choose someone different from your editor. For proofreading, the duties include:

1. Any incorrect line, word, or page spacing - turn on your editing marks feature in your document program to look out for hidden issues.

2. Mismatched items, photos, or graphs.

3. Watch out for widows and orphans - these are short lines, usually of a word or two, that are left alone at the end of a paragraph or the top of a new page. Widows and orphans can diminish readability. The best fix is to make small tweaks in formatting or wording to remove the widows and orphans.[2]

4. Mismatched or awkwardly matched fonts.

5. Consistent use of acronyms and abbreviations.

6. Consistent headers, footers, and page numbers.

7. Accurate table of contents - properly functioning hyperlinks for e-book format, and correct page numbers.[3]

For proofreading, you're just looking for any outward errors, readability, and consistency. Making your book a pleasurable reading experience is the goal of this stage before moving onto publishing.

# PRACTICAL STEPS

Now that you're done writing the manuscript, it's time to polish it up so it's readable. Take your time in this area. Yes, we're shooting to get it all done in forty-eight hours, but don't do it at the expense of quality. Ernest Hemingway said it best, "Write drunk, edit sober."

## GRAMMAR CHECK SOFTWARE

- ○ Use ProWritingAid for grammar and style.
- ○ Edit your manuscript thoroughly.

## EXTERNAL EDITING CONSIDERATION

- ○ Seek unbiased external editing opinions.
- ○ Evaluate editor suggestions critically.

## PROOFREADING FOR PERFECTION

- ○ Scan for spacing, font, and formatting issues.
- ○ Ensure consistency for a polished manuscript.

## NOTES

# Publishing Options

N ot to leave you hanging, I thought I would share a few resources and outlets to release your work. After all, you went through all the steps to make a good book in 48 hours, why not release it to the public and get rewarded for your efforts?

I recommend anyone new to publishing to look into Kindle Direct Publishing (KDP). This company handles print-on-demand and ebook publishing services. When you submit your work, they make it available on their platform and offer other distribution options.

Once they approve your book, and it's live online, customers can order your book fulfilled by KDP. Then you're paid a percentage of the sales, also known as royalties, sixty days after the close of a month.

KDP has exemplary customer service and settled all issues I had in the publishing process. No matter the time of day or night, their customer service reps handled my problems. Also, KDP offers to publish your manuscript as an e-book on Kindle.

According to Forbes, e-books make up 30% of all book sales in the United States, and Amazon has 65% share of that percentage. It's incredible that Amazon provides an easy and inexpensive way for new authors to publish their work.

Take advantage of this opportunity if you want to make even more money from your book project.

Other distributors besides Amazon include IngramSpark, Draft2Digital, Smashwords, and more. Each platform has similar, yet different, publishing systems. Overall, it's fairly simple to learn. These three publishing platforms distribute to major Amazon competitors and other online retailers.

The beauty of these online distributors is it does not cost you a dime to publish your work on their websites. You set up an account through KDP, IngramSpark, Draft2Digital, and Smashwords, for no money. All they expect in return is a percentage of your sales for distributing your work. You lose no rights to your material, and you can always unpublish your book should you want to look into an alternative publishing option.

If you're thinking of publishing your work, I strongly suggest getting a professional book cover design. Though KDP has basic book cover templates, they're generic, don't look very professional and can cheapen your product. I hired many talented graphic designers on Fiverr and usually had excellent service. Search "e-book cover design" on Fiverr and discover many sellers are ready to create a custom cover for a reasonable price. Check out some ones I use frequently at DaleLinks.com/List.

# PRACTICAL STEPS

Now that you put all that work into completing a book in record time, consider the option of self-publishing. Explore a few avenues I mentioned and consider additional options to prep your book for release to the public.

## KDP EXPLORATION

- ○ Research Kindle Direct Publishing (KDP).
- ○ Leverage KDP for print-on-demand and e-books.

## PROFESSIONAL COVER DESIGN

- ○ Prioritize professional book cover design.
- ○ Consider Fiverr for affordable design options.

## NOTES

# Conclusion

Now that we're coming to the end of this short guide, I'll admit to using the same process in writing this book. I'm coming to my last few hours, giving me enough time to read my book, run it through ProWritingAid and send it to be edited by an outside source. As soon as I'm finished proofreading, I'll be ready to publish this manuscript.

You may notice one significant element missing from the process—formatting. I used to use free automated interior formatting by Draft2Digital. The process for formatting is going to be different for some people.

If you have issues with formatting your book properly, do a quick search online for videos or tutorials appropriate to the software you use. Or you can always hire someone on Fiverr to format the book.

Worst-case scenario: KDP offers significant support for formatting your book. Get in touch with KDP by scrolling to the bottom of your KDP dashboard and selecting Contact Us. Also, search on KDP Help for any issues you have because the posts and forums cover common problems.

Whether you have never written a book or need to find a more efficient process in your writing, I sincerely hope you found value in this book. After all, this book is *about* you and *for* you. I have every bit of faith in you and your ability to create beautiful literature for the world to love and enjoy. All you have to do is take massive action, so you can finally realize how you can write your book in 48 hours, starting today!

# PRACTICAL STEPS

We've come to the end of the road. Hopefully, you've followed along and have a completed book. To be clear, the publishing option will most likely take longer than two days. It's merely an avenue worth considering after you've done all your writing. Congratulations and good luck on the success of your upcoming book launch!

## FORMATTING SOLUTIONS:

- ○ Explore automated formatting tools.
- ○ Get support for formatting issues through your preferred publishing platform.

## NOTES

# WRITING CHECKLIST

Consider this checklist your go-to guide for writing your entire book in just 48 hours! It covers everything from planning and writing to fixing mistakes and publishing. Your ultimate checklist to ensure you don't miss a step. Ready to write your book? Let this checklist be your perfect companion!

## PREPARATION

- ◯ Set aside a dedicated time and location.
- ◯ Plan for 90-minute work increments.
- ◯ Minimize distractions and obstacles.

## CONTENT CREATION

- ◯ Choose between typing/writing or voice dictation.
- ◯ Assess typing speed (if typing).
- ◯ Explore typing courses or applications.
- ◯ Consider voice dictation tools.

## CHOOSING YOUR TOPIC

- ◯ Decide between fiction and nonfiction.
- ◯ Identify your passion and strengths.
- ◯ Determine your target audience.

## PICKING A TITLE

- ○ Choose between typing/writing or voice dictation.
- ○ Assess typing speed (if typing).
- ○ Explore typing courses or applications.
- ○ Consider voice dictation tools.

## OUTLINING YOUR BOOK

- ○ List main points for the table of contents.
- ○ Develop key questions for each point.
- ○ For fiction, establish an effective ending and beginning.
- ○ Organize main points into a hierarchy.

## WRITING YOUR BOOK

- ○ Write the first draft without editing.
- ○ Embrace a conversational writing style.
- ○ Channel the flow of thought.

## VOICE-TO-TEXT (OPTIONAL)

- ○ Prepare recording device or speech recognition software.
- ○ Test technology for accurate transcription.
- ○ Speak clearly and spare no details.

## EDIT & PROOFREAD

- ◯ Conduct the first edit using ProWritingAid.
- ◯ Seek an unbiased external editor (if possible).
- ◯ Make corrections based on editor's feedback.
- ◯ Conduct a thorough proofread for errors and consistency.

## PUBLISHING OPTIONS

- ◯ Explore Kindle Direct Publishing (KDP).
- ◯ Consider other distributors like IngramSpark, Draft2Digital, Smashwords.
- ◯ Invest in a professional book cover design.

## MISCELLANEOUS

- ◯ Research formatting options (consider Draft2Digital, Fiverr, or KDP support).

## FINALIZE YOUR BOOK

- ◯ Review the entire manuscript.
- ◯ Run final checks through ProWritingAid.
- ◯ Proofread for any last-minute errors.
- ◯ Publish the manuscript.

# Get More Book Sales

Y ou wrote the book and now it's published. But you're not getting any sales! What gives?

Most people would have you believe self-publishing on Amazon is easy. Why aren't you seeing the results they claim you should get?

Your lack of book sales comes down to 3 culprits:

- Keywords

- Marketing and promotion

- Book reviews

It's time you put all your self-publishing woes to bed and finally increase your book sales for good. Enter *The Amazon Self-Publisher*.

You'll learn:

- The secrets to keyword research and selection

- Cheap yet effective book promotions

- How to get book reviews the legit way

- Where Amazon Advertising will serve your book best

And hundreds of powerful insights! You'll love learning all about Amazon self-publishing, because once you discover proven strategies in self-publishing, your life will change for the good.

Order this 3-part series in 1 book now when you visit...

**DaleLinks.com/SelfPubBook**

# A Small Ask...

N ow that you finished reading this short guide to writing your book in 48 hours, what did you like most about it? Was there something you didn't like?

While you're reflecting on what you read, it'd mean the world to me if you'd leave an honest review from where you got this book. I read all my reviews and am very receptive to candid feedback, so I can improve what I write and publish. Thank you in advance!

-Dale L. Roberts

# About the Author

Meet Dale L. Roberts—he loves helping people share their stories and insights! He's an award-winning author, loves exercising, and makes videos for writers and self-publishers. His YouTube channels have 100,000 subscribers and over 6,000,000 views, cementing his place as the go-to authority in self-publishing.

Dale currently lives with his wife Kelli and cat Izzie in Columbus, Ohio.

Relevant links:

- Website—SelfPublishingWithDale.com

- YouTube—YouTube.com/@DaleLRoberts

- YouTube Podcast—YouTube.com/@SelfPubWithDale

- Twitter—Twitter.com/SelfPubWithDale

* Facebook—Facebook.com/SelfPubWithDale

* Instagram—Instagram.com/SelfPubWithDale

* DON'T GO HERE!—DaleLinks.com

## Also By

*Amazon Keywords for Books* – DaleLinks.com/KeywordsBook
- Maximize your book's reach on Amazon with Dale's guide, unlocking the power of keywords in metadata, descriptions, and AMS ads for online sales success.

*Promotional Strategies for Books* – DaleLinks.com/PromoBook
- Unlock book sales success with Dale's guide—cost-effective marketing strategies, optimal timing, and powerful tips. Transform your book's destiny now.

*Amazon Reviews for Books* – DaleLinks.com/ReviewsBook
- Boost your book's credibility with Dale's guide—learn the value of book review services, find reviewer websites, and master securing editorial reviews. Simplify self-publishing—get it now.

*The Amazon Self Publisher* – DaleLinks.com/SelfPubBook
- Transform your self-publishing success with The Amazon Self-Publisher series—unlocking the secrets to keywords, marketing, and reviews for increased book sales. This compilation includes three award-winning books in *Amazon Keywords for Books*, *Promotional Strategies for Books*, and *Amazon Reviews for Books*.

*Secrets of the Permafree Book* – DaleLinks.com/PermafreeBook
- Boost online sales with a free book on Amazon! Master self-publishing, offer

your book for free, and build an email list to strengthen your online business foundation. Grab the book now to get started!

# Acknowledgements

I'm sending special thanks to my early self-publishing mentor, Jason Bracht. He was instrumental in me writing the first edition of this book.

Also, big thanks to Jeanne De Vita, my writing coach who instilled a stronger understanding of writing—both in nonfiction and fiction. In fact, she's the very reason I revised this manuscript, then discovered I could go deeper on the topic of writing. I'm sitting on a full-length book called How to Write a Nonfiction Book in 24 Hours. I'm sure she'll be the first in line to edit it.

Lastly, I appreciate everyone who has supported me through my YouTube Channels. It felt wrong for me to split my attention between writing and video creation. Once I heard all the success stories and kind words, I knew I didn't have to be ashamed of being an author who produces videos about writing and publishing. You guys are the best!

# References

Introduction

1. Merriam-Webster, Inc. (n.d.). Definition of book. Retrieved on 2015, August 9 from http://www.merriam-webster.com/dictionary/book.

Two Ways to Write Content

1. Literary Rejections. (n.d.). Word Count. Retrieved on 2015, August 9 from http://www.literaryrejections.com/word-count/

2. O'Bannon, Mark. (n.d.) Word Count & Story Length. Retrieved on 2015, August 9 from http://www.betterstorytelling.net/thebasics/storylength.html

3. Sambuchino, Chuck. (2008, November 18). How Long is a Novella? And How Do You Query Agents For Them? Retrieved on 2015, August 9 from http://www.writersdigest.com/editor-blogs/guide-to-literary-agents/qa-from-blog-readers/how-long-is-a-novella-and-how-do-you-query-agents-for-them

4. Sambuchino, Chuck. (2008, November 18). Word Count for Novels and Children's Books: The Definitive Post. Retrieved on 2015, August 9 from http://www.writersdigest.com/editor-blogs/guide-to-literary-agents/word-count-for-novels-and-childrens-books-the-definitive-post

How to Choose Your Topic

1. Merriam-Webster, Inc. (n.d.). Definition of fiction. Retrieved on 2015, August 9 from http://www.merriam-webster.com/dictionary/fiction

2. Merriam-Webster, Inc. (n.d.). Definition of nonfiction. Retrieved on 2015, August 9 from http://www.merriam-webster.com/dictionary/nonfiction

3. Porta, Mandy. (2010, June 22). How to Define Your Target Market. Retrieved on 2015, August 10 from http://www.inc.com/guides/2010/06/defining-your-target-market.html

How to Write Your Book

1. King, Stephen. (2015, February 22). Everything You Need to Know About Writing Successfully – in Ten Minutes. Retrieved on 2015, August 10 from http://www.aerogrammestudio.com/2015/02/24/stephen-king-everything-you-need-to-kno-about-writing-successfully/. Originally printed in *The Writer* magazine circa 1986.

Edit & Proofread Your Book

1. Friedlander, Joel. (2010, January 29). What Every Self-Publisher Ought to Know about Editing. Retrieved on 2015, August 10 from http://www.thebookdesigner.com/2010/01/what-every-self-publisher-ought-to-know-about-editing/

2. Strizver, Ilene. (n.d.). Rags, Widows & Orphans. Retrieved on 2015, August 10 from http://www.fonts.com/content/learning/fontology/level-2/text-typography/rags-widows-orphans

3. Friedlander, Joel. (2010, January 29). What Every Self-Publisher Ought to Know about Editing. Retrieved on 2015, August 10 from http://www.thebookdesigner.com/2010/01/what-every-self-publisher-ought-to-know-about-editing/

Made in the USA
Las Vegas, NV
11 June 2024

90967063R00046